PRESIDENTS OF THE *United States*

Joe BIDEN

46th

Tamara L. Britton

Big Buddy Books
An Imprint of Abdo Publishing
abdobooks.com

Published by Abdo Publishing, a division of ABDO, PO Box 398166, Minneapolis, Minnesota 55439.

Printed in the United States of America, North Mankato, Minnesota
112024
012025

Cover Photo: Wikimedia Commons
Interior Photos: AP Images (pp. 6, 13, 15, 19, 21, 23); Getty (pp. 27, 29); Shutterstock (pp. 7, 17, 25); Wikimedia Commons (pp. 5, 6, 9, 11)

Editor: Lauri Nelson
Designers: Candice Keimig and Laura Graphenteen

Library of Congress Control Number: 2023949382

Publisher's Cataloging-in-Publication Data

Names: Britton, Tamara L., author.
Title: Joe Biden / by Tamara L. Britton
Description: Minneapolis, Minnesota : Abdo Publishing, 2025 | Series: Presidents of the United States | Includes online resources and index.
Identifiers: ISBN 9781098294496 (lib. bdg.) | ISBN 9798384914228 (ebook)
Subjects: LCSH: Biden, Joseph R., Jr.--Juvenile literature. | Presidents--Juvenile literature. | Presidents--United States--History--Juvenile literature. | Legislators--United States--Biography--Juvenile literature. | Politics and government--Biography--Juvenile literature.
Classification: DDC 973.93--dc23

CONTENTS

JOE BIDEN

Joe Biden was elected the forty-sixth president of the United States in 2020. He was 77 years old. He was the nation's oldest president. Biden was also the first to have a woman vice president.

Before becoming president, Biden worked in the US Senate. He served as vice president under President Barack Obama. People trusted Biden's experience.

As president, Biden led the country during a difficult time. He fought to control a worldwide illness and save the US **economy**. Biden worked to bring unity to the nation.

Joe Biden

TIMELINE

1942

On November 20, Joe Biden was born in Scranton, Pennsylvania.

1965

Biden **graduated** from college.

1966

Biden married Neilia Hunter.

1972
Biden was elected to the US Senate; his wife and daughter were killed in a car accident.

1977
Biden married Jill Tracy Jacobs.

2009
On January 20, Barack Obama was **inaugurated** president; Biden became vice president.

2021
On January 20, Joe Biden was inaugurated the forty-sixth US president.

2024
Biden supported Kamala Harris in her run for president.

YOUNG JOEY

Joseph Robinette Biden Jr. was born on November 20, 1942, in Scranton, Pennsylvania. His family called him Joey. Joey was the oldest of Joseph Robinette Biden Sr. and Catherine Biden's four children.

★ ★ ★ ★ ★ *Fast* FACTS ★ ★ ★ ★ ★

BORN: November 20, 1942

WIVES: Neilia Hunter (1942–1972), Jill Tracy Jacobs (1951–)

CHILDREN: four

POLITICAL PARTY: Democrat

AGE AT INAUGURATION: 78

YEARS SERVED: 2021–2025

VICE PRESIDENT: Kamala Harris

As a child, Joey stuttered. He often repeated the first syllable of his last name. This led his classmates to call him "Bye-Bye."

EDUCATION

In 1952, Biden's family moved to Delaware. There, he attended Archmere Academy. To help pay his **tuition**, Biden got a job washing the school's windows and taking care of its grounds.

Biden **graduated** in 1961 and entered the University of Delaware. He studied history and political science.

Biden graduated from college in 1965. He then started law school at Syracuse University in Syracuse, New York. He graduated in 1968.

At Archmere, Biden *(center)* was elected class president. He also played wide receiver and halfback on the school's football team.

FAMILY MAN

In his third year at the University of Delaware, Biden met Neilia Hunter. They married in 1966. When Biden finished law school, the couple moved to Wilmington, Delaware. There, Biden worked as a lawyer.

Joe and Neilia soon welcomed children. Their first son, Joseph R. Biden III, was born in 1969. The family called him Beau. In 1970, Robert Hunter Biden, called Hunter, was born. A year later, the couple welcomed a daughter, Naomi.

Biden with his wife Neilia and sons, Hunter *(left)* and Beau *(right)*

ENTERING POLITICS

At age 29, Biden ran for a seat in the US Senate. In his campaign, Biden spoke of his support for the **environment** and **civil rights**. He opposed the **Vietnam War**. On November 7, 1972, he won the election.

Soon after Biden's victory, tragedy struck. On December 18, 1972, his wife and children were in a traffic accident. Beau and Hunter were badly hurt. Neilia and Naomi died.

Biden considered delaying his career. But he decided to honor his commitment. Biden was sworn in on January 5, 1973, at the hospital where his sons were recovering.

Biden is the longest-serving Delaware senator in history. He was reelected six times and served for 36 years.

A SECOND CHANCE

In 1975, Biden met Jill Tracy Jacobs. Two years later, they were married. Their daughter, Ashley, was born in 1981.

Biden ran for president in the 1988 election. During the campaign, he had painful headaches. His doctors found that he had two brain **aneurysms**. He dropped out of the race.

Biden underwent surgeries to remove the aneurysms. He also had surgery for **blood clots** in his lungs. He returned to work in the Senate in September 1988.

Biden and his wife Jill on the campaign trail in 1987

SENATOR BIDEN

In 1987, Biden served on the Committee on the **Judiciary**. He helped write the Violent Crime Control and Law Enforcement Act of 1994 and the Violence Against Women Act.

During the 1990s, Biden worked to end a war in the **Balkans**. He also helped expand the **North Atlantic Treaty Organization**.

Biden served on the Foreign Relations Committee in 2001. While he worked hard in the Senate, he had not given up on his dream of becoming the US president.

DID YOU KNOW?

Biden is the sixth-youngest person ever elected to the US Senate.

Senator Biden argued in the Foreign Relations Committee against the US position on South Africa's system of racial segregation.

VICE PRESIDENT

Biden ran for president again in 2008. But other candidates received more **primary** votes. So, he dropped out of the race.

Barack Obama won the **Democratic nomination**. He asked Biden to be his **running mate**. On January 20, 2009, they were sworn in. Four years later, they were reelected.

Vice President Biden worked on the New START nuclear arms treaty. He **negotiated** an **economic** bill. He also worked to reduce gun violence, end cancer, and bring troops home from Iraq.

Vice President Biden applauds as President Barack Obama signs executive orders to control gun violence.

THE 2020 ELECTION

Biden left office in 2017. Then, he launched his third campaign for president in 2019. Biden chose California senator Kamala Harris as his **running mate**.

The campaign had some challenges. A virus called COVID-19 spread across the world. Efforts to stop it hurt the US **economy**.

The country also faced protests calling for an end to **racism** and violence against Black Americans. The next president would lead a country suffering in many ways.

Kamala Harris's first name comes from an ancient Indian language word for lotus flower.

Text UNITED to 30330

BIDEN
HARRIS

On November 3, 2020, over 60 million people went to the polls. Due to COVID-19, more than 100 million voted early or by mail. On November 7, Biden and Harris were named the winners.

Some Americans claimed there had been cheating in the election. On January 6, 2021, some of them gathered in Washington, DC. Some stormed the US Capitol. In the months following, more than 700 protesters plead guilty for the crimes they committed.

On January 20, 2021, Joe Biden was **inaugurated**. He became the oldest US president. Kamala Harris became the first woman and first Black vice president.

President BIDEN'S CABINET

January 20, 2021 - January 20, 2025

- ★ **STATE:** Antony Blinken
- ★ **TREASURY:** Dr. Janet Yellen
- ★ **DEFENSE:** Lloyd Austin
- ★ **ATTORNEY GENERAL:** Merrick Garland
- ★ **INTERIOR:** Deb Haaland
- ★ **AGRICULTURE:** Tom Vilsack
- ★ **COMMERCE:** Gina Raimondo
- ★ **LABOR:** Marty Walsh, Julie Su (from March 11, 2023)
- ★ **HEALTH AND HUMAN SERVICES:** Xavier Becerra
- ★ **HOUSING AND URBAN DEVELOPMENT:** Marcia Fudge, Adrianne Todman (from March 22, 2024)
- ★ **TRANSPORTATION:** Pete Buttigieg
- ★ **ENERGY:** Jennifer Granholm
- ★ **EDUCATION:** Dr. Miguel Cardona
- ★ **VETERANS AFFAIRS:** Denis McDonough
- ★ **HOMELAND SECURITY:** Alejandro Mayorkas

PRESIDENT BIDEN

President Biden worked to bring the country together. He created laws that helped the American people survive the pandemic. Biden lowered the cost of gas, energy, and health care. He created more jobs and raised pay for American workers.

In 2021, President Biden made Juneteenth a national holiday. Juneteenth is short for "June Nineteenth." The holiday celebrates the end of slavery in America. It was the first new holiday since Martin Luther King Jr. Day in 1983.

President Biden signs the law making Juneteenth the 12th national holiday. Opal Lee *(left)*, the "Grandmother of Juneteenth," looks on.

Biden worked to improve the US **economy**. He addressed problems with the **environment**. Biden also led world leaders to support the people of Ukraine after their country was invaded by Russia in February of 2022.

Later in 2022, Supreme Court Justice Stephen Breyer retired. President Biden kept his campaign promise to **nominate** a Black woman to the Supreme Court. He chose Ketanji Brown Jackson, who became the first Black woman to serve on the country's highest court.

President Biden served just one term. He decided not to run for reelection. Biden did what he thought was right for the country.

Biden called Justice Jackson "one of the nation's brightest legal minds." After being sworn in, she was one of four women serving together on the nine-member court for the first time in history.

OFFICE OF THE PRESIDENT

Branches of Government

The US government has three branches. They are the executive, legislative, and judicial branches. Each branch has some power over the others. This is called a system of checks and balances.

★ Executive Branch

The executive branch enforces laws. It is made up of the president, the vice president, and the president's cabinet. The president represents the United States around the world. He or she also signs bills into law and leads the military.

★ Legislative Branch

The legislative branch makes laws, maintains the military, and regulates trade. It also has the power to declare war. This branch includes the Senate and the House of Representatives. Together, these two houses form Congress.

★ Judicial Branch

The judicial branch interprets laws. It is made up of district courts, courts of appeals, and the Supreme Court. District courts try cases. Sometimes people disagree with a trial's outcome. Then he or she may appeal. If a court of appeals supports the ruling, a person may appeal to the Supreme Court.

Qualifications for Office

To be president, a candidate must be at least 35 years old. The person must be a natural-born US citizen. He or she must also have lived in the United States for at least 14 years.

Electoral College

The US presidential election is an indirect election. Voters from each state choose electors. These electors represent their state in the Electoral College. Each elector has one electoral vote. Electors cast their vote for the candidate with the highest number of votes from people in their state. A candidate must receive the majority of Electoral College votes to win.

Term of Office

Each president may be elected to two four-year terms. The presidential election is held on the Tuesday after the first Monday in November. The president is sworn in on January 20 of the following year. At that time, he or she takes the oath of office.

It states:

> I do solemnly swear (or affirm) that I will faithfully execute the office of President of the United States, and will to the best of my ability, preserve, protect and defend the Constitution of the United States.

Line of Succession

The Presidential Succession Act of 1947 states who becomes president if the president cannot serve. The vice president is first in the line. Next are the Speaker of the House and the President Pro Tempore of the Senate. It may happen that none of these individuals is able to serve. Then the office falls to the president's cabinet members. They would take office in the order in which each department was created:

1. **Vice President**
2. **Speaker of the House**
3. **President Pro Tempore of the Senate**
4. **Secretary of State**
5. **Secretary of the Treasury**
6. **Secretary of Defense**
7. **Attorney General**
8. **Secretary of the Interior**
9. **Secretary of Agriculture**
10. **Secretary of Commerce**
11. **Secretary of Labor**
12. **Secretary of Health and Human Services**
13. **Secretary of Housing and Urban Development**
14. **Secretary of Transportation**
15. **Secretary of Energy**
16. **Secretary of Education**
17. **Secretary of Veterans Affairs**
18. **Secretary of Homeland Security**

Modern-Day Benefits

- ★ While in office, the president receives a salary. It is $400,000 per year. He or she lives in the White House. The president also has 24-hour Secret Service protection.
- ★ The president may travel on a Boeing 747 jet. This special jet is called Air Force One. It can hold 76 passengers. It has kitchens, a dining room, sleeping areas, and more. Air Force One can fly halfway around the world before needing to refuel. It can even refuel in flight!
- ★ When the president travels by car, he or she uses Cadillac One. It is a Cadillac that has been modified. The car has heavy armor and communications systems. The president may even take Cadillac One along when visiting other countries.
- ★ The president also travels on a helicopter. It is called Marine One. It may also be taken along when the president visits other countries.
- ★ Sometimes the president needs to get away with family and friends. Camp David is the official presidential retreat. It is located in Maryland. The US Navy maintains the retreat. The US Marine Corps keeps it secure. The camp offers swimming, tennis, golf, and hiking.
- ★ When the president leaves office, he or she receives lifetime Secret Service protection. He or she also receives a yearly pension that may be modified by Congress every year. In 2023, the pension amount was $226,300. The former president also receives money for office space, supplies, and staff.

PRESIDENTS AND THEIR TERMS

PRESIDENT	PARTY	TOOK OFFICE	LEFT OFFICE	TERMS SERVED	VICE PRESIDENT
George Washington	None	April 30, 1789	March 4, 1797	Two	John Adams
John Adams	Federalist	March 4, 1797	March 4, 1801	One	Thomas Jefferson
Thomas Jefferson	Democratic-Republican	March 4, 1801	March 4, 1809	Two	Aaron Burr, George Clinton
James Madison	Democratic-Republican	March 4, 1809	March 4, 1817	Two	George Clinton, Elbridge Gerry
James Monroe	Democratic-Republican	March 4, 1817	March 4, 1825	Two	Daniel D. Tompkins
John Quincy Adams	Democratic-Republican	March 4, 1825	March 4, 1829	One	John C. Calhoun
Andrew Jackson	Democrat	March 4, 1829	March 4, 1837	Two	John C. Calhoun, Martin Van Buren
Martin Van Buren	Democrat	March 4, 1837	March 4, 1841	One	Richard M. Johnson
William H. Harrison	Whig	March 4, 1841	April 4, 1841	Died During First Term	John Tyler
John Tyler	Whig	April 6, 1841	March 4, 1845	Completed Harrison's Term	Office Vacant
James K. Polk	Democrat	March 4, 1845	March 4, 1849	One	George M. Dallas
Zachary Taylor	Whig	March 5, 1849	July 9, 1850	Died During First Term	Millard Fillmore

PRESIDENT	PARTY	TOOK OFFICE	LEFT OFFICE	TERMS SERVED	VICE PRESIDENT
Millard Fillmore	Whig	July 10, 1850	March 4, 1853	Completed Taylor's Term	Office Vacant
Franklin Pierce	Democrat	March 4, 1853	March 4, 1857	One	William R.D. King
James Buchanan	Democrat	March 4, 1857	March 4, 1861	One	John C. Breckinridge
Abraham Lincoln	Republican	March 4, 1861	April 15, 1865	Served One Term, Died During Second Term	Hannibal Hamlin, Andrew Johnson
Andrew Johnson	Democrat	April 15, 1865	March 4, 1869	Completed Lincoln's Second Term	Office Vacant
Ulysses S. Grant	Republican	March 4, 1869	March 4, 1877	Two	Schuyler Colfax, Henry Wilson
Rutherford B. Hayes	Republican	March 3, 1877	March 4, 1881	One	William A. Wheeler
James A. Garfield	Republican	March 4, 1881	September 19, 1881	Died During First Term	Chester Arthur
Chester Arthur	Republican	September 20, 1881	March 4, 1885	Completed Garfield's Term	Office Vacant
Grover Cleveland	Democrat	March 4, 1885	March 4, 1889	One	Thomas A. Hendricks
Benjamin Harrison	Republican	March 4, 1889	March 4, 1893	One	Levi P. Morton
Grover Cleveland	Democrat	March 4, 1893	March 4, 1897	One	Adlai E. Stevenson
William McKinley	Republican	March 4, 1897	September 14, 1901	Served One Term, Died During Second Term	Garret A. Hobart, Theodore Roosevelt

PRESIDENT	PARTY	TOOK OFFICE	LEFT OFFICE	TERMS SERVED	VICE PRESIDENT
Theodore Roosevelt	Republican	September 14, 1901	March 4, 1909	Completed McKinley's Second Term, Served One Term	Office Vacant, Charles Fairbanks
William Taft	Republican	March 4, 1909	March 4, 1913	One	James S. Sherman
Woodrow Wilson	Democrat	March 4, 1913	March 4, 1921	Two	Thomas R. Marshall
Warren G. Harding	Republican	March 4, 1921	August 2, 1923	Died During First Term	Calvin Coolidge
Calvin Coolidge	Republican	August 3, 1923	March 4, 1929	Completed Harding's Term, Served One Term	Office Vacant, Charles Dawes
Herbert Hoover	Republican	March 4, 1929	March 4, 1933	One	Charles Curtis
Franklin D. Roosevelt	Democrat	March 4, 1933	April 12, 1945	Served Three Terms, Died During Fourth Term	John Nance Garner, Henry A. Wallace, Harry S. Truman
Harry S. Truman	Democrat	April 12, 1945	January 20, 1953	Completed Roosevelt's Fourth Term, Served One Term	Office Vacant, Alben Barkley
Dwight D. Eisenhower	Republican	January 20, 1953	January 20, 1961	Two	Richard Nixon
John F. Kennedy	Democrat	January 20, 1961	November 22, 1963	Died During First Term	Lyndon B. Johnson
Lyndon B. Johnson	Democrat	November 22, 1963	January 20, 1969	Completed Kennedy's Term, Served One Term	Office Vacant, Hubert H. Humphrey
Richard Nixon	Republican	January 20, 1969	August 9, 1974	Completed First Term, Resigned During Second Term	Spiro T. Agnew, Gerald Ford

PRESIDENT	PARTY	TOOK OFFICE	LEFT OFFICE	TERMS SERVED	VICE PRESIDENT
Gerald Ford	Republican	August 9, 1974	January 20, 1977	Completed Nixon's Second Term	Nelson A. Rockefeller
Jimmy Carter	Democrat	January 20, 1977	January 20, 1981	One	Walter Mondale
Ronald Reagan	Republican	January 20, 1981	January 20, 1989	Two	George H.W. Bush
George H.W. Bush	Republican	January 20, 1989	January 20, 1993	One	Dan Quayle
Bill Clinton	Democrat	January 20, 1993	January 20, 2001	Two	Al Gore
George W. Bush	Republican	January 20, 2001	January 20, 2009	Two	Dick Cheney
Barack Obama	Democrat	January 20, 2009	January 20, 2017	Two	Joe Biden
Donald Trump	Republican	January 20, 2017	January 20, 2021	One	Mike Pence
Joe Biden	Democrat	January 20, 2021	January 20, 2025	One	Kamala Harris
Donald Trump	Republican	January 20, 2025			JD Vance

★ ★ WRITE TO THE *President* ★ ★

You may write to the president at:
The White House
1600 Pennsylvania Avenue NW
Washington, DC 20500

You may e-mail the president at:
www.whitehouse.gov/contact

"Our future cannot depend on the government alone. The ultimate solutions lie in the attitudes and the actions of the American people."

Joe Biden

GLOSSARY

aneurysm (AN-u-rizm)—a bulge in a blood vessel.

Balkans—the countries occupying the Balkan Peninsula.

blood clot—a thick and sticky clump of blood that stops blood flow.

civil rights—the rights of a citizen, such as the right to vote or freedom of speech.

Democrat—a member of the Democratic political party.

economy—the way that a country produces, sells, and buys goods and services.

environment—the natural world, including air, land, water, animals, and plants.

graduate (GRA-juh-wayt)—to complete a level of schooling.

inaugurate (ih-NAW-gyuh-rayt)—to swear into a political office.

judiciary (joo-DIH-shee-ehr-ee)—the branch of government in charge of courts and judges.

negotiate—to discuss something formally in order to come to an agreement.

nominate—to name as a possible winner.

North Atlantic Treaty Organization—a group formed by the United States, Canada, and some European countries in 1949. It tries to create peace among its nations and protect them from common enemies.

primary—a method of selecting candidates to run for public office. A political party holds an election among its own members to select the party members who will represent it in the coming general election.

racism (RAY-sih-zuhm)—the belief that one race is better than another.

running mate—someone running for vice president with another person running for president in an election.

tuition (tuh-WIH-shuhn)—money students pay to attend school.

Vietnam War—a war that took place between South Vietnam and North Vietnam from 1957 to 1975. The United States was involved in this war for many years.

WEBSITES

To learn more about Joe Biden, please visit **abdobooklinks.com** or scan this QR code. These links are routinely monitored and updated to provide the most current information available.

INDEX